KATHERINE WOLKOFF

LOUISE GLÜCK

FAITHFUL AND VIRTUOUS NIGHT

LOUISE GLÜCK is the author of thirteen books of poems and a collection of essays. Her many awards include the Pulitzer Prize, the National Book Award, the National Book Critics Circle Award, the Bollingen Prize for Poetry, and the Wallace Stevens Award from the Academy of American Poets. She teaches at Yale University and lives in Cambridge, Massachusetts.

FAITHFUL AND VIRTUOUS NIGHT

FAITHFUL AND VIRTUOUS NIGHT

LOUISE GLÜCK

FARRAR, STRAUS AND GIROUX

NEW YORK

FARRAR, STRAUS AND GIROUX
18 West 18th Street, New York 10011

Printed in the United States of America
Published in 2014 by Farrar, Straus and Giroux
First paperback edition, 2015

Grateful acknowledgment is made to the following publications, in which some of
these poems first appeared: *The American Scholar*, *The New Republic*, *The New York Review of Books*,
The New York Times, *The New Yorker*, *Poetry*, and *The Threepenny Review*.

The Library of Congress has cataloged the hardcover edition as follows:
Glück, Louise, 1943–
[Poems. Selections]
Faithful and virtuous night / Louise Glück. — First edition.
pages   cm
ISBN 978-0-374-15201-7 (Hardcover)
I. Title

PS3557.L8 A6 2014
811'.54—dc23

2013048984

Paperback ISBN: 978-0-374-53577-3

Designed by Gretchen Achilles

Farrar, Straus and Giroux books may be purchased for educational, business, or promotional use.
For information on bulk purchases, please contact the Macmillan Corporate and Premium Sales Department
at 1-800-221-7945, extension 5442, or write to specialmarkets@macmillan.com.

www.fsgbooks.com
www.twitter.com/fsgbooks • www.facebook.com/fsgbooks

7   9   10   8

CONTENTS

FAITHFUL AND VIRTUOUS NIGHT

PARABLE

First divesting ourselves of worldly goods, as St. Francis teaches,
in order that our souls not be distracted
by gain and loss, and in order also
that our bodies be free to move
easily at the mountain passes, we had then to discuss
whither or where we might travel, with the second question being
should we have a purpose, against which
many of us argued fiercely that such purpose
corresponded to worldly goods, meaning a limitation or constriction,
whereas others said it was by this word we were consecrated
pilgrims rather than wanderers: in our minds, the word translated as
a dream, a something-sought, so that by concentrating we might see it
glimmering among the stones, and not
pass blindly by; each
further issue we debated equally fully, the arguments going back and forth,
so that we grew, some said, less flexible and more resigned,
like soldiers in a useless war. And snow fell upon us, and wind blew,
which in time abated—where the snow had been, many flowers appeared,
and where the stars had shone, the sun rose over the tree line
so that we had shadows again; many times this happened.
Also rain, also flooding sometimes, also avalanches, in which
some of us were lost, and periodically we would seem
to have achieved an agreement, our canteens
hoisted upon our shoulders; but always that moment passed, so
(after many years) we were still at that first stage, still
preparing to begin a journey, but we were changed nevertheless;
we could see this in one another; we had changed although
we never moved, and one said, ah, behold how we have aged, traveling
from day to night only, neither forward nor sideward, and this seemed

in a strange way miraculous. And those who believed we should have a
   purpose
believed this was the purpose, and those who felt we must remain free
in order to encounter truth felt it had been revealed.

AN ADVENTURE

1.

It came to me one night as I was falling asleep
that I had finished with those amorous adventures
to which I had long been a slave. Finished with love?
my heart murmured. To which I responded that many profound
    discoveries
awaited us, hoping, at the same time, I would not be asked
to name them. For I could not name them. But the belief that they
    existed—
surely this counted for something?

2.

The next night brought the same thought,
this time concerning poetry, and in the nights that followed
various other passions and sensations were, in the same way,
set aside forever, and each night my heart
protested its future, like a small child being deprived of a favorite toy.
But these farewells, I said, are the way of things.
And once more I alluded to the vast territory
opening to us with each valediction. And with that phrase I became
a glorious knight riding into the setting sun, and my heart
became the steed underneath me.

3.

I was, you will understand, entering the kingdom of death,
though why this landscape was so conventional
I could not say. Here, too, the days were very long
while the years were very short. The sun sank over the far mountain.
The stars shone, the moon waxed and waned. Soon
faces from the past appeared to me:

my mother and father, my infant sister; they had not, it seemed,
finished what they had to say, though now
I could hear them because my heart was still.

4.
At this point, I attained the precipice
but the trail did not, I saw, descend on the other side;
rather, having flattened out, it continued at this altitude
as far as the eye could see, though gradually
the mountain that supported it completely dissolved
so that I found myself riding steadily through the air—
All around, the dead were cheering me on, the joy of finding them
obliterated by the task of responding to them—

5.
As we had all been flesh together,
now we were mist.
As we had been before objects with shadows,
now we were substance without form, like evaporated chemicals.
Neigh, neigh, said my heart,
or perhaps nay, nay—it was hard to know.

6.
Here the vision ended. I was in my bed, the morning sun
contentedly rising, the feather comforter
mounded in white drifts over my lower body.
You had been with me—
there was a dent in the second pillowcase.
We had escaped from death—
or was this the view from the precipice?

THE PAST

Small light in the sky appearing
suddenly between
two pine boughs, their fine needles

now etched onto the radiant surface
and above this
high, feathery heaven—

Smell the air. That is the smell of the white pine,
most intense when the wind blows through it
and the sound it makes equally strange,
like the sound of the wind in a movie—

Shadows moving. The ropes
making the sound they make. What you hear now
will be the sound of the nightingale, *chordata*,
the male bird courting the female—

The ropes shift. The hammock
sways in the wind, tied
firmly between two pine trees.

Smell the air. That is the smell of the white pine.

It is my mother's voice you hear
or is it only the sound the trees make
when the air passes through them

because what sound would it make,
passing through nothing?

FAITHFUL AND VIRTUOUS NIGHT

My story begins very simply: I could speak and I was happy.
Or: I could speak, thus I was happy.
Or: I was happy, thus speaking.
I was like a bright light passing through a dark room.

If it is so difficult to begin, imagine what it will be to end—
On my bed, sheets printed with colored sailboats
conveying, simultaneously, visions of adventure (in the form of exploration)
and sensations of gentle rocking, as of a cradle.

Spring, and the curtains flutter.
Breezes enter the room, bringing the first insects.
A sound of buzzing like the sound of prayers.

Constituent
memories of a large memory.
Points of clarity in a mist, intermittently visible,
like a lighthouse whose one task
is to emit a signal.

But what really is the point of the lighthouse?
This is north, it says.
Not: I am your safe harbor.

Much to his annoyance, I shared this room with my older brother.
To punish me for existing, he kept me awake, reading
adventure stories by the yellow nightlight.

The habits of long ago: my brother on his side of the bed,
subdued but voluntarily so,
his bright head bent over his hands, his face obscured—

At the time of which I'm speaking,
my brother was reading a book he called
the faithful and virtuous night.
Was this the night in which he read, in which I lay awake?
No—it was a night long ago, a lake of darkness in which
a stone appeared, and on the stone
a sword growing.

Impressions came and went in my head,
a faint buzz, like the insects.
When not observing my brother, I lay in the small bed we shared
staring at the ceiling—never
my favorite part of the room. It reminded me
of what I couldn't see, the sky obviously, but more painfully
my parents sitting on the white clouds in their white travel outfits.

And yet I too was traveling,
in this case imperceptibly
from that night to the next morning,
and I too had a special outfit:
striped pyjamas.

Picture if you will a day in spring.
A harmless day: my birthday.
Downstairs, three gifts on the breakfast table.

In one box, pressed handkerchiefs with a monogram.
In the second box, colored pencils arranged
in three rows, like a school photograph.
In the last box, a book called *My First Reader*.

My aunt folded the printed wrapping paper;
the ribbons were rolled into neat balls.
My brother handed me a bar of chocolate
wrapped in silver paper.

Then, suddenly, I was alone.

Perhaps the occupation of a very young child
is to observe and listen:

In that sense, everyone was occupied—
I listened to the various sounds of the birds we fed,
the tribes of insects hatching, the small ones
creeping along the windowsill, and overhead
my aunt's sewing machine drilling
holes in a pile of dresses—

Restless, are you restless?
Are you waiting for day to end, for your brother to return to his book?
For night to return, faithful, virtuous,
repairing, briefly, the schism between
you and your parents?

This did not, of course, happen immediately.
Meanwhile, there was my birthday;
somehow the luminous outset became
the interminable middle.

Mild for late April. Puffy
clouds overhead, floating among the apple trees.
I picked up *My First Reader*, which appeared to be
a story about two children—I could not read the words.

On page three, a dog appeared.
On page five, there was a ball—one of the children
threw it higher than seemed possible, whereupon
the dog floated into the sky to join the ball.
That seemed to be the story.

I turned the pages. When I was finished
I resumed turning, so the story took on a circular shape,
like the zodiac. It made me dizzy. The yellow ball

seemed promiscuous, equally
at home in the child's hand and the dog's mouth—

Hands underneath me, lifting me.
They could have been anyone's hands,
a man's, a woman's.
Tears falling on my exposed skin. Whose tears?
Or were we out in the rain, waiting for the car to come?

The day had become unstable.
Fissures appeared in the broad blue, or,
more precisely, sudden black clouds
imposed themselves on the azure background.

Somewhere, in the far backward reaches of time,
my mother and father
were embarking on their last journey,
my mother fondly kissing the new baby, my father
throwing my brother into the air.

I sat by the window, alternating
my first lesson in reading with
watching time pass, my introduction to
philosophy and religion.

Perhaps I slept. When I woke
the sky had changed. A light rain was falling,
making everything very fresh and new—

I continued staring
at the dog's frantic reunions
with the yellow ball, an object
soon to be replaced
by another object, perhaps a soft toy—

And then suddenly evening had come.
I heard my brother's voice
calling to say he was home.

How old he seemed, older than this morning.
He set his books beside the umbrella stand
and went to wash his face.
The cuffs of his school uniform
dangled below his knees.

You have no idea how shocking it is
to a small child when
something continuous stops.

The sounds, in this case, of the sewing room,
like a drill, but very far away—

Vanished. Silence was everywhere.
And then, in the silence, footsteps.
And then we were all together, my aunt and my brother.

Then tea was set out.
At my place, a slice of ginger cake
and at the center of the slice,
one candle, to be lit later.
How quiet you are, my aunt said.

It was true—
sounds weren't coming out of my mouth. And yet
they were in my head, expressed, possibly,
as something less exact, thought perhaps,
though at the time they still seemed like sounds to me.

Something was there where there had been nothing.
Or should I say, nothing was there
but it had been defiled by questions—

Questions circled my head; they had a quality
of being organized in some way, like planets—

Outside, night was falling. Was this
that lost night, star-covered, moonlight-spattered,
like some chemical preserving
everything immersed in it?

My aunt had lit the candle.

Darkness overswept the land
and on the sea the night floated
strapped to a slab of wood—

If I could speak, what would I have said?
I think I would have said
goodbye, because in some sense
it *was* goodbye—

Well, what could I do? I wasn't
a baby anymore.

I found the darkness comforting.
I could see, dimly, the blue and yellow
sailboats on the pillowcase.

I was alone with my brother;
we lay in the dark, breathing together,
the deepest intimacy.

It had occurred to me that all human beings are divided
into those who wish to move forward
and those who wish to go back.
Or you could say, those who wish to keep moving
and those who want to be stopped in their tracks
as by the blazing sword.

My brother took my hand.
Soon it too would be floating away
though perhaps, in my brother's mind,
it would survive by becoming imaginary—

Having finally begun, how does one stop?
I suppose I can simply wait to be interrupted
as in my parents' case by a large tree—
the barge, so to speak, will have passed
for the last time between the mountains.
Something, they say, like falling asleep,
which I proceeded to do.

The next day, I could speak again.
My aunt was overjoyed—
it seemed my happiness had been
passed on to her, but then
she needed it more, she had two children to raise.

I was content with my brooding.
I spent my days with the colored pencils
(I soon used up the darker colors)
though what I saw, as I told my aunt,
was less a factual account of the world
than a vision of its transformation
subsequent to passage through the void of myself.

Something, I said, like the world in spring.

When not preoccupied with the world
I drew pictures of my mother
for which my aunt posed,
holding, at my request,
a twig from a sycamore.

As to the mystery of my silence:
I remained puzzled
less by my soul's retreat than
by its return, since it returned empty-handed—

How deep it goes, this soul,
like a child in a department store,
seeking its mother—

Perhaps it is like a diver
with only enough air in his tank
to explore the depths for a few minutes or so—
then the lungs send him back.

But something, I was sure, opposed the lungs,
possibly a death wish—
(I use the word *soul* as a compromise).

Of course, in a certain sense I was not empty-handed:
I had my colored pencils.
In another sense, that is my point:
I had accepted substitutes.

It was challenging to use the bright colors,
the ones left, though my aunt preferred them of course—
she thought all children should be lighthearted.

And so time passed: I became
a boy like my brother, later
a man.

I think here I will leave you. It has come to seem
there is no perfect ending.
Indeed, there are infinite endings.
Or perhaps, once one begins,
there are only endings.

THEORY OF MEMORY

Long, long ago, before I was a tormented artist, afflicted with longing yet incapable of forming durable attachments, long before this, I was a glorious ruler uniting all of a divided country—so I was told by the fortune-teller who examined my palm. Great things, she said, are ahead of you, or perhaps behind you; it is difficult to be sure. And yet, she added, what is the difference? Right now you are a child holding hands with a fortune-teller. All the rest is hypothesis and dream.

A SHARPLY WORDED SILENCE

Let me tell you something, said the old woman.
We were sitting, facing each other,
in the park at _____, a city famous for its wooden toys.

At the time, I had run away from a sad love affair,
and as a kind of penance or self-punishment, I was working
at a factory, carving by hand the tiny hands and feet.

The park was my consolation, particularly in the quiet hours
after sunset, when it was often abandoned.
But on this evening, when I entered what was called the Contessa's Garden,
I saw that someone had preceded me. It strikes me now
I could have gone ahead, but I had been
set on this destination; all day I had been thinking of the cherry trees
with which the glade was planted, whose time of blossoming had nearly ended.

We sat in silence. Dusk was falling,
and with it came a feeling of enclosure
as in a train cabin.

When I was young, she said, I liked walking the garden path at twilight
and if the path was long enough I would see the moon rise.
That was for me the great pleasure: not sex, not food, not worldly amusement.
I preferred the moon's rising, and sometimes I would hear,
at the same moment, the sublime notes of the final ensemble
of *The Marriage of Figaro*. Where did the music come from?
I never knew.

Because it is the nature of garden paths
to be circular, each night, after my wanderings,
I would find myself at my front door, staring at it,
barely able to make out, in darkness, the glittering knob.

It was, she said, a great discovery, albeit my real life.

But certain nights, she said, the moon was barely visible through the clouds
and the music never started. A night of pure discouragement.
And still the next night I would begin again, and often all would be well.

I could think of nothing to say. This story, so pointless as I write it out,
was in fact interrupted at every stage with trance-like pauses
and prolonged intermissions, so that by this time night had started.

Ah the capacious night, the night
so eager to accommodate strange perceptions. I felt that some important secret
was about to be entrusted to me, as a torch is passed
from one hand to another in a relay.

My sincere apologies, she said.
I had mistaken you for one of my friends.
And she gestured toward the statues we sat among,
heroic men, self-sacrificing saintly women
holding granite babies to their breasts.
Not changeable, she said, like human beings.

I gave up on them, she said.
But I never lost my taste for circular voyages.
Correct me if I'm wrong.

Above our heads, the cherry blossoms had begun
to loosen in the night sky, or maybe the stars were drifting,
drifting and falling apart, and where they landed
new worlds would form.

Soon afterward I returned to my native city
and was reunited with my former lover.
And yet increasingly my mind returned to this incident,
studying it from all perspectives, each year more intensely convinced,
despite the absence of evidence, that it contained some secret.
I concluded finally that whatever message there might have been
was not contained in speech—so, I realized, my mother used to speak to me,
her sharply worded silences cautioning me and chastising me—

and it seemed to me I had not only returned to my lover
but was now returning to the Contessa's Garden
in which the cherry trees were still blooming
like a pilgrim seeking expiation and forgiveness,

so I assumed there would be, at some point,
a door with a glittering knob,
but when this would happen and where I had no idea.

VISITORS FROM ABROAD

1.

Sometime after I had entered
that time of life
people prefer to allude to in others
but not in themselves, in the middle of the night
the phone rang. It rang and rang
as though the world needed me,
though really it was the reverse.

I lay in bed, trying to analyze
the ring. It had
my mother's persistence and my father's
pained embarrassment.

When I picked it up, the line was dead.
Or was the phone working and the caller dead?
Or was it not the phone, but the door perhaps?

2.

My mother and father stood in the cold
on the front steps. My mother stared at me,
a daughter, a fellow female.
You never think of us, she said.

We read your books when they reach heaven.
Hardly a mention of us anymore, hardly a mention of your sister.
And they pointed to my dead sister, a complete stranger,
tightly wrapped in my mother's arms.

But for us, she said, you wouldn't exist.
And your sister—you have your sister's soul.
After which they vanished, like Mormon missionaries.

3.
The street was white again,
all the bushes covered with heavy snow
and the trees glittering, encased with ice.

I lay in the dark, waiting for the night to end.
It seemed the longest night I had ever known,
longer than the night I was born.

I write about you all the time, I said aloud.
Every time I say "I," it refers to you.

4.
Outside the street was silent.
The receiver lay on its side among the tangled sheets;
its peevish throbbing had ceased some hours before.

I left it as it was,
its long cord drifting under the furniture.

I watched the snow falling,
not so much obscuring things
as making them seem larger than they were.

Who would call in the middle of the night?
Trouble calls, despair calls.
Joy is sleeping like a baby.

ABORIGINAL LANDSCAPE

You're stepping on your father, my mother said,
and indeed I was standing exactly in the center
of a bed of grass, mown so neatly it could have been
my father's grave, although there was no stone saying so.

You're stepping on your father, she repeated,
louder this time, which began to be strange to me,
since she was dead herself; even the doctor had admitted it.

I moved slightly to the side, to where
my father ended and my mother began.

The cemetery was silent. Wind blew through the trees;
I could hear, very faintly, sounds of weeping several rows away,
and beyond that, a dog wailing.

At length these sounds abated. It crossed my mind
I had no memory of being driven here,
to what now seemed a cemetery, though it could have been
a cemetery in my mind only; perhaps it was a park, or if not a park,
a garden or bower, perfumed, I now realized, with the scent of roses—
douceur de vivre filling the air, the sweetness of living,
as the saying goes. At some point,

it occurred to me I was alone.
Where had the others gone,
my cousins and sister, Caitlin and Abigail?

By now the light was fading. Where was the car
waiting to take us home?

I then began seeking for some alternative. I felt
an impatience growing in me, approaching, I would say, anxiety.
Finally, in the distance, I made out a small train,
stopped, it seemed, behind some foliage, the conductor
lingering against a doorframe, smoking a cigarette.

Do not forget me, I cried, running now
over many plots, many mothers and fathers—

Do not forget me, I cried, when at last I reached him.
Madam, he said, pointing to the tracks,
surely you realize this is the end, the tracks do not go farther.
His words were harsh, and yet his eyes were kind;
this encouraged me to press my case harder.
But they go back, I said, and I remarked
their sturdiness, as though they had many such returns ahead of them.

You know, he said, our work is difficult: we confront
much sorrow and disappointment.
He gazed at me with increasing frankness.
I was like you once, he added, in love with turbulence.

Now I spoke as to an old friend:
What of you, I said, since he was free to leave,
have you no wish to go home,
to see the city again?

This is my home, he said.
The city—the city is where I disappear.

When the train stops, the woman said, you must get on it. But how will I know, the child asked, it is the right train? It will be the right train, said the woman, because it is the right time. A train approached the station; clouds of grayish smoke streamed from the chimney. How terrified I am, the child thinks, clutching the yellow tulips she will give to her grandmother. Her hair has been tightly braided to withstand the journey. Then, without a word, she gets on the train, from which a strange sound comes, not in a language like the one she speaks, something more like a moan or a cry.

CORNWALL

A word drops into the mist
like a child's ball into high grass
where it remains seductively
flashing and glinting until
the gold bursts are revealed to be
simply field buttercups.

Word / mist, word / mist: thus it was with me.
And yet, my silence was never total—

Like a curtain rising on a vista,
sometimes the mist cleared: alas, the game was over.
The game was over and the word had been
somewhat flattened by the elements
so it was now both recovered and useless.

I was renting, at the time, a house in the country.
Fields and mountains had replaced tall buildings.
Fields, cows, sunsets over the damp meadow.
Night and day distinguished by rotating birdcalls,
the busy murmurs and rustlings merging into
something akin to silence.

I sat, I walked about. When night came,
I went indoors. I cooked modest dinners for myself
by the light of candles.
Evenings, when I could, I wrote in my journal.

Far, far away I heard cowbells
crossing the meadow.
The night grew quiet in its way.
I sensed the vanished words
lying with their companions,
like fragments of an unclaimed biography.

It was all, of course, a great mistake.
I was, I believed, facing the end:
like a fissure in a dirt road,
the end appeared before me—

as though the tree that confronted my parents
had become an abyss shaped like a tree, a black hole
expanding in the dirt, where by day
a simple shadow would have done.

It was, finally, a relief to go home.

When I arrived, the studio was filled with boxes.
Cartons of tubes, boxes of the various
objects that were my still lives,
the vases and mirrors, the blue bowl
I filled with wooden eggs.

As to the journal:
I tried. I persisted.
I moved my chair onto the balcony—

The streetlights were coming on,
lining the sides of the river.
The offices were going dark.
At the river's edge,
fog encircled the lights;
one could not, after a while, see the lights
but a strange radiance suffused the fog,
its source a mystery.

The night progressed. Fog
swirled over the lit bulbs.
I suppose that is where it was visible;
elsewhere, it was simply the way things were,
blurred where they had been sharp.

I shut my book.
It was all behind me, all in the past.

Ahead, as I have said, was silence.

I spoke to no one.
Sometimes the phone rang.

Day alternated with night, the earth and sky
taking turns being illuminated.

AFTERWORD

Reading what I have just written, I now believe
I stopped precipitously, so that my story seems to have been
slightly distorted, ending, as it did, not abruptly
but in a kind of artificial mist of the sort
sprayed onto stages to allow for difficult set changes.

Why did I stop? Did some instinct
discern a shape, the artist in me
intervening to stop traffic, as it were?

A shape. Or fate, as the poets say,
intuited in those few long-ago hours—

I must have thought so once.
And yet I dislike the term
which seems to me a crutch, a phase,
the adolescence of the mind, perhaps—

Still, it was a term I used myself,
frequently to explain my failures.
Fate, destiny, whose designs and warnings
now seem to me simply
local symmetries, metonymic
baubles within immense confusion—

Chaos was what I saw.
My brush froze—I could not paint it.

Darkness, silence: that was the feeling.

What did we call it then?
A "crisis of vision" corresponding, I believed,
to the tree that confronted my parents,

but whereas they were forced
forward into the obstacle,
I retreated or fled—

Mist covered the stage (my life).
Characters came and went, costumes were changed,
my brush hand moved side to side
far from the canvas,
side to side, like a windshield wiper.

Surely this was the desert, the dark night.
(In reality, a crowded street in London,
the tourists waving their colored maps.)

One speaks a word: *I*.
Out of this stream
the great forms—

I took a deep breath. And it came to me
the person who drew that breath
was not the person in my story, his childish hand
confidently wielding the crayon—

Had I been that person? A child but also
an explorer to whom the path is suddenly clear, for whom
the vegetation parts—

And beyond, no longer screened from view, that exalted
solitude Kant perhaps experienced
on his way to the bridges—
(We share a birthday.)

Outside, the festive streets
were strung, in late January, with exhausted Christmas lights.
A woman leaned against her lover's shoulder
singing Jacques Brel in her thin soprano—

Bravo! the door is shut.
Now nothing escapes, nothing enters—

I hadn't moved. I felt the desert
stretching ahead, stretching (it now seems)
on all sides, shifting as I speak,

so that I was constantly
face-to-face with blankness, that
stepchild of the sublime,

which, it turns out,
has been both my subject and my medium.

What would my twin have said, had my thoughts
reached him?

Perhaps he would have said
in my case there was no obstacle (for the sake of argument)
after which I would have been

referred to religion, the cemetery where
questions of faith are answered.

The mist had cleared. The empty canvases
were turned inward against the wall.

The little cat is dead (so the song went).

Shall I be raised from death, the spirit asks.
And the sun says yes.
And the desert answers
your voice is sand scattered in wind.

MIDNIGHT

At last the night surrounded me;
I floated on it, perhaps in it,
or it carried me as a river carries
a boat, and at the same time
it swirled above me,
star-studded but dark nevertheless.

These were the moments I lived for.
I was, I felt, mysteriously lifted above the world
so that action was at last impossible
which made thought not only possible but limitless.

It had no end. I did not, I felt,
need to do anything. Everything
would be done for me, or done to me,
and if it was not done, it was not
essential.

I was on my balcony.
In my right hand I held a glass of Scotch
in which two ice cubes were melting.

Silence had entered me.
It was like the night, and my memories—they were like stars
in that they were fixed, though of course
if one could see as do the astronomers
one would see they are unending fires, like the fires of hell.
I set my glass on the iron railing.

Below, the river sparkled. As I said,
everything glittered—the stars, the bridge lights, the important
illumined buildings that seemed to stop at the river
then resume again, man's work
interrupted by nature. From time to time I saw
the evening pleasure boats; because the night was warm,
they were still full.

This was the great excursion of my childhood.
The short train ride culminating in a gala tea by the river,
then what my aunt called our promenade,
then the boat itself that cruised back and forth over the dark water—

The coins in my aunt's hand passed into the hand of the captain.
I was handed my ticket, each time a fresh number.
Then the boat entered the current.

I held my brother's hand.
We watched the monuments succeeding one another
always in the same order
so that we moved into the future
while experiencing perpetual recurrences.

The boat traveled up the river and then back again.
It moved through time and then
through a reversal of time, though our direction
was forward always, the prow continuously
breaking a path in the water.

It was like a religious ceremony
in which the congregation stood
awaiting, beholding,
and that was the entire point, the beholding.

The city drifted by,
half on the right side, half on the left.

See how beautiful the city is,
my aunt would say to us. Because
it was lit up, I expect. Or perhaps because
someone had said so in the printed booklet.

Afterward we took the last train.
I often slept, even my brother slept.
We were country children, unused to these intensities.
You boys are spent, my aunt said,
as though our whole childhood had about it
an exhausted quality.
Outside the train, the owl was calling.

How tired we were when we reached home.
I went to bed with my socks on.

The night was very dark.
The moon rose.
I saw my aunt's hand gripping the railing.

In great excitement, clapping and cheering,
the others climbed onto the upper deck
to watch the land disappear into the ocean—

THE SWORD IN THE STONE

My analyst looked up briefly.
Naturally I couldn't see him
but I had learned, in our years together,
to intuit these movements. As usual,
he refused to acknowledge
whether or not I was right. My ingenuity versus
his evasiveness: our little game.

At such moments, I felt the analysis
was flourishing: it seemed to bring out in me
a sly vivaciousness I was
inclined to repress. My analyst's
indifference to my performances
was now immensely soothing. An intimacy

had grown up between us
like a forest around a castle.

The blinds were closed. Vacillating
bars of light advanced across the carpeting.
Through a small strip above the windowsill,
I saw the outside world.

All this time I had the giddy sensation
of floating above my life. Far away
that life occurred. But was it
still occurring: that was the question.

Late summer: the light was fading.
Escaped shreds flickered over the potted plants.

The analysis was in its seventh year.
I had begun to draw again—
modest little sketches, occasional
three-dimensional constructs
modeled on functional objects—

And yet, the analysis required
much of my time. From what
was this time deducted: that
was also the question.

I lay, watching the window,
long intervals of silence alternating
with somewhat listless ruminations
and rhetorical questions—

My analyst, I felt, was watching me.
So, in my imagination, a mother stares at her sleeping child,
forgiveness preceding understanding.

Or, more likely, so my brother must have gazed at me—
perhaps the silence between us prefigured
this silence, in which everything that remained unspoken
was somehow shared. It seemed a mystery.

Then the hour was over.

I descended as I had ascended;
the doorman opened the door.

The mild weather of the day had held.
Above the shops, striped awnings had unfurled
protecting the fruit.

Restaurants, shops, kiosks
with late newspapers and cigarettes.
The insides grew brighter
as the outside grew darker.

Perhaps the drugs were working?
At some point, the streetlights came on.

I felt, suddenly, a sense of cameras beginning to turn;
I was aware of movement around me, my fellow beings
driven by a mindless fetish for action—

How deeply I resisted this!
It seemed to me shallow and false, or perhaps
partial and false—
Whereas truth—well, truth as I saw it
was expressed as stillness.

I walked awhile, staring into the windows of the galleries—
my friends had become famous.

I could hear the river in the background,
from which came the smell of oblivion
interlaced with potted herbs from the restaurants—

I had arranged to join an old acquaintance for dinner.
There he was at our accustomed table;
the wine was poured; he was engaged with the waiter,
discussing the lamb.

As usual, a small argument erupted over dinner, ostensibly
concerning aesthetics. It was allowed to pass.

Outside, the bridge glittered.
Cars rushed back and forth, the river
glittered back, imitating the bridge. Nature
reflecting art: something to that effect.
My friend found the image potent.

He was a writer. His many novels, at the time,
were much praised. One was much like another.
And yet his complacency disguised suffering
as perhaps my suffering disguised complacency.
We had known each other many years.

Once again, I had accused him of laziness.
Once again, he flung the word back—

He raised his glass and turned it upside-down.
This is your purity, he said,
this is your perfectionism—
The glass was empty; it left no mark on the tablecloth.

The wine had gone to my head.
I walked home slowly, brooding, a little drunk.
The wine had gone to my head, or was it
the night itself, the sweetness at the end of summer?

It is the critics, he said,
the critics have the ideas. We artists
(he included me)—we artists
are just children at our games.

After the orchestra had been playing for some time, and had passed the andante, the scherzo, the poco adagio, and the first flautist had put his head on the stand because he would not be needed until tomorrow, there came a passage that was called the forbidden music because it could not, the composer specified, be played. And still it must exist and be passed over, an interval at the discretion of the conductor. But tonight, the conductor decides, it must be played—he has a hunger to make his name. The flautist wakes with a start. Something has happened to his ears, something he has never felt before. His sleep is over. Where am I now, he thinks. And then he repeated it, like an old man lying on the floor instead of in his bed. Where am I now?

An elderly writer had formed the habit of writing the words THE END on a piece of paper before he began his stories, after which he would gather a stack of pages, typically thin in winter when the daylight was brief, and comparatively dense in summer when his thought became again loose and associative, expansive like the thought of a young man. Regardless of their number, he would place these blank pages over the last, thus obscuring it. Only then would the story come to him, chaste and refined in winter, more free in summer. By these means he had become an acknowledged master.

He worked by preference in a room without clocks, trusting the light to tell him when the day was finished. In summer, he liked the window open. How then, in summer, did the winter wind enter the room? You are right, he cried out to the wind, this is what I have lacked, this decisiveness and abruptness, this surprise—O, if I could do this I would be a god! And he lay on the cold floor of the study watching the wind stirring the pages, mixing the written and unwritten, the end among them.

I had an assistant, but he was melancholy,
so melancholy it interfered with his duties.
He was to open my letters, which were few,
and answer those that required answers,
leaving a space at the bottom for my signature.
And under my signature, his own initials,
in which formality, at the outset, he took great pride.
When the phone rang, he was to say
his employer was at the moment occupied,
and offer to convey a message.

After several months, he came to me.
Master, he said (which was his name for me),
I have become useless to you; you must turn me out.
And I saw that he had packed his bags
and was prepared to go, though it was night
and the snow was falling. My heart went out to him.
Well, I said, if you cannot perform these few duties,
what can you do? And he pointed to his eyes,
which were full of tears. I can weep, he said.
Then you must weep for me, I told him,
as Christ wept for mankind.

Still he was hesitant.
Your life is enviable, he said;
what must I think of when I cry?
And I told him of the emptiness of my days,
and of time, which was running out,
and of the meaninglessness of my achievement,

and as I spoke I had the odd sensation
of once more feeling something
for another human being—

He stood completely still.
I had lit a small fire in the fireplace;
I remember hearing the contented murmurs of the dying logs—

Master, he said, you have given
meaning to my suffering.

It was a strange moment.
The whole exchange seemed both deeply fraudulent
and profoundly true, as though such words as emptiness and
    meaninglessness
had stimulated some remembered emotion
which now attached itself to this occasion and person.

His face was radiant. His tears glinted
red and gold in the firelight.
Then he was gone.

Outside the snow was falling,
the landscape changing into a series
of bland generalizations
marked here and there with enigmatic
shapes where the snow had drifted.
The street was white, the various trees were white—
Changes of the surface, but is that not really
all we ever see?

I found the stairs somewhat more difficult than I had expected and so I sat down, so to speak, in the middle of the journey. Because there was a large window opposite the railing, I was able to entertain myself with the little dramas and comedies of the street outside, though no one I knew passed by, no one, certainly, who could have assisted me. Nor were the stairs themselves in use, as far as I could see. You must get up, my lad, I told myself. Since this seemed suddenly impossible, I did the next best thing: I prepared to sleep, my head and arms on the stair above, my body crouched below. Sometime after this, a little girl appeared at the top of the staircase, holding the hand of an elderly woman. Grandmother, cried the little girl, there is a dead man on the staircase! We must let him sleep, said the grandmother. We must walk quietly by. He is at that point in life at which neither returning to the beginning nor advancing to the end seems bearable; therefore, he has decided to stop, here, in the midst of things, though this makes him an obstacle to others, such as ourselves. But we must not give up hope; in my own life, she continued, there was such a time, though that was long ago. And here, she let her granddaughter walk in front of her so they could pass me without disturbing me.

I would have liked to hear the whole of her story, since she seemed, as she passed by, a vigorous woman, ready to take pleasure in life, and at the same time forthright, without illusions. But soon their voices faded into whispers, or they were far away. Will we see him when we return, the child murmured. He will be long gone by then, said her grandmother, he will have finished climbing up or down, as the case may be. Then I will say goodbye now, said the little girl. And she knelt below me, chanting a prayer I recognized as the Hebrew prayer for the dead. Sir, she whispered, my grandmother tells me you are not dead, but I thought perhaps this would soothe you in your terrors, and I will not be here to sing it at the right time.

When you hear this again, she said, perhaps the words will be less intimidating, if you remember how you first heard them, in the voice of a little girl.

APPROACH OF THE HORIZON

One morning I awoke unable to move my right arm.
I had, periodically, suffered from considerable
pain on that side, in my painting arm,
but in this instance there was no pain.
Indeed, there was no feeling.

My doctor arrived within the hour.
There was immediately the question of other doctors,
various tests, procedures—
I sent the doctor away
and instead hired the secretary who transcribes these notes,
whose skills, I am assured, are adequate to my needs.
He sits beside the bed with his head down,
possibly to avoid being described.

So we begin. There is a sense
of gaiety in the air,
as though birds were singing.
Through the open window come gusts of sweet scented air.

My birthday (I remember) is fast approaching.
Perhaps the two great moments will collide
and I will see my selves meet, coming and going—
Of course, much of my original self
is already dead, so a ghost would be forced
to embrace a mutilation.

The sky, alas, is still far away,
not really visible from the bed.
It exists now as a remote hypothesis,

a place of freedom utterly unconstrained by reality.
I find myself imagining the triumphs of old age,
immaculate, visionary drawings
made with my left hand—
"left," also, as "remaining."

The window is closed. Silence again, multiplied.
And in my right arm, all feeling departed.
As when the stewardess announces the conclusion
of the audio portion of one's in-flight service.

Feeling has departed—it occurs to me
this would make a fine headstone.

But I was wrong to suggest
this has occurred before.
In fact, I have been hounded by feeling;
it is the gift of expression
that has so often failed me.
Failed me, tormented me, virtually all my life.

The secretary lifts his head,
filled with the abstract deference
the approach of death inspires.
It cannot help, really, but be thrilling,
this emerging of shape from chaos.

A machine, I see, has been installed by my bed
to inform my visitors
of my progress toward the horizon.

My own gaze keeps drifting toward it,
the unstable line gently
ascending, descending,
like a human voice in a lullaby.

And then the voice grows still.
At which point my soul will have merged
with the infinite, which is represented
by a straight line,
like a minus sign.

I have no heirs
in the sense that I have nothing of substance
to leave behind.
Possibly time will revise this disappointment.
Those who know me well will find no news here;
I sympathize. Those to whom
I am bound by affection
will forgive, I hope, the distortions
compelled by the occasion.

I will be brief. This concludes,
as the stewardess says,
our short flight.

And all the persons one will never know
crowd into the aisle, and all are funneled
into the terminal.

THE WHITE SERIES

One day continuously followed another.
Winter passed. The Christmas lights came down
together with the shabby stars
strung across the various shopping streets.
Flower carts appeared on the wet pavements,
the metal pails filled with quince and anemones.

The end came and went.
Or should I say, at intervals the end approached;
I passed through it like a plane passing through a cloud.
On the other side, the vacant sign still glowed above the lavatory.

My aunt died. My brother moved to America.

On my wrist, the watch face glistened in the false darkness
(the movie was being shown).
This was its special feature, a kind of bluish throbbing
which made the numbers easy to read, even in the absence of light.
Princely, I always thought.

And yet the serene transit of the hour hand
no longer represented my perception of time
which had become a sense of immobility
expressed as movement across vast distances.

The hand moved;
the twelve, as I watched, became the one again.

Whereas time was now this environment in which
I was contained with my fellow passengers,
as the infant is contained in his sturdy crib
or, to stretch the point, as the unborn child
wallows in his mother's womb.

Outside the womb, the earth had fallen away;
I could see flares of lightning striking the wing.

When my funds were gone,
I went to live for a while
in a small house on my brother's land
in the state of Montana.

I arrived in darkness;
at the airport, my bags were lost.

It seemed to me I had moved
not horizontally but rather from a very low place
to something very high,
perhaps still in the air.

Indeed, Montana was like the moon—
My brother drove confidently over the icy road,
from time to time stopping to point out
some rare formation.

We were, in the main, silent.
It came to me we had resumed
the arrangements of childhood,
our legs touching, the steering wheel
now substituting for the book.

And yet, in the deepest sense, they were interchangeable:
had not my brother always been steering,
both himself and me, out of our bleak bedroom
into a night of rocks and lakes
punctuated with swords sticking up here and there—

The sky was black. The earth was white and cold.

I watched the night fading. Above the white snow
the sun rose, turning the snow a strange pinkish color.

Then we arrived.
We stood awhile in the cold hall, waiting for the heat to start.
My brother wrote down my list of groceries.
Across my brother's face,
waves of sadness alternated with waves of joy.

I thought, of course, of the house in Cornwall.
The cows, the monotonous summery music of the bells—

I felt, as you will guess, an instant of stark terror.

And then I was alone.
The next day, my bags arrived.

I unpacked my few belongings.
The photograph of my parents on their wedding day
to which was now added
a photograph of my aunt in her aborted youth, a souvenir
she had cherished and passed on to me.

Beyond these, only toiletries and medications,
together with my small collection of winter clothes.

My brother brought me books and journals.
He taught me various new world skills
for which I would soon have no use.

And yet this was to me the new world:
there was nothing, and nothing was supposed to happen.
The snow fell. Certain afternoons,
I gave drawing lessons to my brother's wife.

At some point, I began to paint again.

It was impossible to form
any judgment of the work's value.
Suffice to say the paintings were
immense and entirely white. The paint had been
applied thickly, in great irregular strokes—

Fields of white and glimpses, flashes
of blue, the blue of the western sky,
or what I called to myself
watch-face blue. It spoke to me of another world.

I have led my people, it said,
into the wilderness
where they will be purified.

My brother's wife would stand mesmerized.
Sometimes my nephew came
(he would soon become my life companion).
I see, she would say, the face of a child.

She meant, I think, that feelings emanated from the surface,
feelings of helplessness or desolation—

Outside, the snow was falling.
I had been, I felt, accepted into its stillness.
And at the same time, each stroke was a decision,
not a conscious decision, but a decision nevertheless,
as when, for example, the murderer pulls the trigger.

This, he is saying. This is what I mean to do.
Or perhaps, what I need to do.
Or, this is all I can do.
Here, I believe, the analogy ends
in a welter of moral judgments.

Afterward, I expect, he remembers nothing.
In the same way, I cannot say exactly
how these paintings came into being, though in the end
there were many of them, difficult to ship home.

When I returned, Harry was with me.
He is, I believe, a gentle boy
with a taste for domesticity.
In fact, he has taught himself to cook
despite the pressures of his academic schedule.

We suit each other. Often he sings as he goes about his work.
So my mother sang (or, more likely, so my aunt reported).
I request, often, some particular song to which I am attached,
and he goes about learning it. He is, as I say,
an obliging boy. The hills are alive, he sings,
over and over. And sometimes, in my darker moods,
the Jacques Brel which has haunted me.

The little cat is dead, meaning, I suppose,
one's last hope.

The cat is dead, Harry sings,
he will be pointless without his body.
In Harry's voice, it is deeply soothing.

Sometimes his voice shakes, as with great emotion,
and then for a while the hills are alive overwhelms
the cat is dead.

But we do not, in the main, need to choose between them.

Still, the darker songs inspire him; each verse acquires variations.

The cat is dead: who will press, now,
his heart over my heart to warm me?

The end of hope, I think it means,
and yet in Harry's voice it seems a great door is swinging open—

The snow-covered cat disappears in the high branches;
O what will I see when I follow?

Once there was a horse, and on the horse there was a rider. How handsome they looked in the autumn sunlight, approaching a strange city! People thronged the streets or called from the high windows. Old women sat among flowerpots. But when you looked about for another horse or another rider, you looked in vain. My friend, said the animal, why not abandon me? Alone, you can find your way here. But to abandon you, said the other, would be to leave a part of myself behind, and how can I do that when I do not know which part you are?

As I turned over the last page, after many nights, a wave of sorrow enveloped me. Where had they all gone, these people who had seemed so real? To distract myself, I walked out into the night; instinctively, I lit a cigarette. In the dark, the cigarette glowed, like a fire lit by a survivor. But who would see this light, this small dot among the infinite stars? I stood awhile in the dark, the cigarette glowing and growing small, each breath patiently destroying me. How small it was, how brief. Brief, brief, but inside me now, which the stars could never be.

THE STORY OF A DAY

1.

I was awakened this morning as usual
by the narrow bars of light coming through the blinds
so that my first thought was that the nature of light
was incompleteness—

I pictured the light as it existed before the blinds stopped it—
how thwarted it must be, like a mind
dulled by too many drugs.

2.

I soon found myself
at my narrow table; to my right,
the remains of a small meal.

Language was filling my head, wild exhilaration
alternated with profound despair—

But if the essence of time is change,
how can anything become nothing?
This was the question I asked myself.

3.

Long into the night I sat brooding at my table
until my head was so heavy and empty
I was compelled to lie down.
But I did not lie down. Instead, I rested my head on my arms
which I had crossed in front of me on the bare wood.
Like a fledgling in a nest, my head
lay on my arms.

It was the dry season.
I heard the clock tolling, three, then four—

I began at this point to pace the room
and shortly afterward the streets outside
whose turns and windings were familiar to me
from nights like this. Around and around I walked,
instinctively imitating the hands of the clock.
My shoes, when I looked down, were covered with dust.

By now the moon and stars had faded.
But the clock was still glowing in the church tower—

4.
Thus I returned home.
I stood a long time
on the stoop where the stairs ended,
refusing to unlock the door.

The sun was rising.
The air had become heavy,
not because it had greater substance
but because there was nothing left to breathe.

I closed my eyes.
I was torn between a structure of oppositions
and a narrative structure—

5.
The room was as I left it.
There was the bed in the corner.
There was the table under the window.

There was the light battering itself against the window
until I raised the blinds
at which point it was redistributed
as flickering among the shade trees.

A SUMMER GARDEN

I.
Several weeks ago I discovered a photograph of my mother
sitting in the sun, her face flushed as with achievement or triumph.
The sun was shining. The dogs
were sleeping at her feet where time was also sleeping,
calm and unmoving as in all photographs.

I wiped the dust from my mother's face.
Indeed, dust covered everything; it seemed to me the persistent
haze of nostalgia that protects all relics of childhood.
In the background, an assortment of park furniture, trees, and shrubbery.

The sun moved lower in the sky, the shadows lengthened and darkened.
The more dust I removed, the more these shadows grew.
Summer arrived. The children
leaned over the rose border, their shadows
merging with the shadows of the roses.

A word came into my head, referring
to this shifting and changing, these erasures
that were now obvious—

it appeared, and as quickly vanished.
Was it blindness or darkness, peril, confusion?

Summer arrived, then autumn. The leaves turning,
the children bright spots in a mash of bronze and sienna.

2.

When I had recovered somewhat from these events,
I replaced the photograph as I had found it
between the pages of an ancient paperback,
many parts of which had been
annotated in the margins, sometimes in words but more often
in spirited questions and exclamations
meaning "I agree" or "I'm unsure, puzzled"—

The ink was faded. Here and there I couldn't tell
what thoughts occurred to the reader
but through the blotches I could sense
urgency, as though tears had fallen.

I held the book awhile.
It was *Death in Venice* (in translation);
I had noted the page in case, as Freud believed,
nothing is an accident.

Thus the little photograph
was buried again, as the past is buried in the future.
In the margin there were two words,
linked by an arrow: "sterility" and, down the page, "oblivion"—

"And it seemed to him the pale and lovely
Summoner out there smiled at him and beckoned . . ."

3.

How quiet the garden is;
no breeze ruffles the Cornelian cherry.
Summer has come.

How quiet it is
now that life has triumphed. The rough

pillars of the sycamores
support the immobile
shelves of the foliage,

the lawn beneath
lush, iridescent—

And in the middle of the sky,
the immodest god.

Things are, he says. They are, they do not change;
response does not change.

How hushed it is, the stage
as well as the audience; it seems
breathing is an intrusion.

He must be very close,
the grass is shadowless.

How quiet it is, how silent,
like an afternoon in Pompeii.

4.

Mother died last night,
Mother who never dies.

Winter was in the air,
many months away
but in the air nevertheless.

It was the tenth of May.
Hyacinth and apple blossom
bloomed in the back garden.

We could hear
Maria singing songs from Czechoslovakia—

How alone I am—
songs of that kind.

How alone I am,
no mother, no father—
my brain seems so empty without them.

Aromas drifted out of the earth;
the dishes were in the sink,
rinsed but not stacked.

Under the full moon
Maria was folding the washing;
the stiff sheets became
dry white rectangles of moonlight.

How alone I am, but in music
my desolation is my rejoicing.

It was the tenth of May
as it had been the ninth, the eighth.

Mother slept in her bed,
her arms outstretched, her head
balanced between them.

5.
Beatrice took the children to the park in Cedarhurst.
The sun was shining. Airplanes
passed back and forth overhead, peaceful because the war was over.

It was the world of her imagination:
true and false were of no importance.

Freshly polished and glittering—
that was the world. Dust
had not yet erupted on the surface of things.

The planes passed back and forth, bound
for Rome and Paris—you couldn't get there
unless you flew over the park. Everything
must pass through, nothing can stop—

The children held hands, leaning
to smell the roses.
They were five and seven.

Infinite, infinite—that
was her perception of time.

She sat on a bench, somewhat hidden by oak trees.
Far away, fear approached and departed;
from the train station came the sound it made.

The sky was pink and orange, older because the day was over.

There was no wind. The summer day
cast oak-shaped shadows on the green grass.

A man walks alone in the park and beside him a woman walks, also alone. How does one know? It is as though a line exists between them, like a line on a playing field. And yet, in a photograph they might appear a married couple, weary of each other and of the many winters they have endured together. At another time, they might be strangers about to meet by accident. She drops her book; stooping to pick it up, she touches, by accident, his hand and her heart springs open like a child's music box. And out of the box comes a little ballerina made of wood. I have created this, the man thinks; though she can only whirl in place, still she is a dancer of some kind, not simply a block of wood. This must explain the puzzling music coming from the trees.